The
United States Presidents

THOMAS JEFFERSON

ABDO Publishing Company

Heidi M.D. Elston

visit us at
www.abdopublishing.com

Published by ABDO Publishing Company, 8000 West 78th Street, Edina, Minnesota 55439.
Copyright © 2009 by Abdo Consulting Group, Inc. International copyrights reserved in all
countries. No part of this book may be reproduced in any form without written permission from the
publisher. The Checkerboard Library™ is a trademark and logo of ABDO Publishing Company.

Printed in the United States.

Cover Photo: Getty Images
Interior Photos: Alamy pp. 9, 14, 25; AP Images p. 10; Corbis pp. 11, 17, 18, 19, 23;
    Getty Images pp. 12, 27, 28; iStockphoto pp. 13, 29, 32; National Archives pp. 16, 21, 22, 26;
    North Wind p. 15; Picture History pp. 5, 20

Editor: Megan M. Gunderson
Art Direction & Cover Design: Neil Klinepier
Interior Design: Jaime Martens

Library of Congress Cataloging-in-Publication Data

Elston, Heidi M.D., 1979-
  Thomas Jefferson / Heidi M.D. Elston.
     p. cm. -- (The United States presidents)
  Includes index.
  ISBN 978-1-60453-460-3
  1. Jefferson, Thomas, 1743-1826--Juvenile literature. 2. Presidents--United States--Biography--
Juvenile literature. I. Title.

  E332.79.E54 2009
  973.4'6092092--dc22
  [B]
                                        2008027054

CONTENTS

THOMAS JEFFERSON

Thomas Jefferson was the third president of the United States. He helped create America. Jefferson also fought for human rights.

Jefferson was born in Virginia. There, he served as a legislator and as governor. Jefferson also worked in the U.S. government. He served as minister to France, **secretary of state**, and vice president. In addition, he helped form the Democratic-Republican Party.

In 1776, Jefferson wrote the Declaration of Independence. This document declared that the United States was a new, independent country.

Jefferson began his first term as president in 1801. Through the purchase of the Louisiana Territory, he doubled the size of the United States. Then, he sent explorers west to learn about this land.

President Jefferson served two terms. He then returned to Monticello, his home in Virginia. During his retirement, Jefferson founded the University of Virginia in Charlottesville. He designed the school's buildings. He even picked the books for the library!

4

Throughout his life, Jefferson worked hard for freedom of religion and freedom of speech. These are important rights in the United States. He also supported the arts, sciences, and education. And, he worked for equal rights for all Americans. For this reason, Thomas Jefferson is sometimes called "Man of the People."

TIMELINE

1743 - On April 13, Thomas Jefferson was born in Shadwell, Virginia.

1768 - Jefferson began work on his home that became known as Monticello.

1772 - On January 1, Jefferson married Martha Wayles Skelton.

1773 - In Massachusetts's Boston Harbor, the Boston Tea Party occurred.

1775 - Jefferson attended the Second Continental Congress.

1776 - Jefferson was the chief author of the Declaration of Independence.

1777 - Jefferson wrote the Virginia Statute for Religious Freedom.

1779 - The people of Virginia elected Jefferson to his first term as governor.

1782 - On September 6, Martha Jefferson died.

1784 - Jefferson traveled to France as a diplomat.

1785 - Jefferson became U.S. minister to France.

1789–1793 - Jefferson served as the first U.S. secretary of state.

1796 - Jefferson became vice president under John Adams.

1801–1809 - Jefferson served as the third president of the United States.

1803 - Jefferson purchased the Louisiana Territory.

1815 - Jefferson sold his personal library to Congress.

1819 - Jefferson started the University of Virginia, which opened six years later.

1826 - On July 4, Thomas Jefferson died at Monticello.

When Thomas Jefferson was born, England's North American colonies used the Julian calendar. On that calendar, Jefferson's birthday was April 2. In 1752, England and its colonies adopted the Gregorian calendar. Then, April 2 became April 13.

Jefferson was the first president to start a term in the new White House. Former president John Adams had lived there for just a few months before his term ended.

President Jefferson had a pet mockingbird. He let it fly around the White House when he did not have guests.

Jefferson's grandson, James Randolph, was the first child born in the White House.

Jefferson appears on the U.S. nickel.

EARLY YEARS

Thomas Jefferson was born in Shadwell, Virginia, on April 13, 1743. At the time, Virginia was a British colony.

Thomas was the oldest son of Peter Jefferson and Jane Randolph Jefferson. Peter had many jobs, including making maps of the Virginia wilderness. Jane was from one of the most well-known families in Virginia. She cared for her eight children.

In 1745, the Jefferson family moved to a nearby plantation. Virginia had no public schools at that time. So, Thomas learned lessons from a **tutor** until 1752. That year, his family returned to Shadwell.

Thomas continued his education at boarding schools. He enjoyed learning. He liked reading, as well as languages and music. Thomas played the violin, sang, and danced. He also spent time in nature, memorizing the names of trees and plants.

FAST FACTS

BORN - April 13, 1743
WIFE - Martha Wayles Skelton (1748–1782)
CHILDREN - 6
POLITICAL PARTY - Democratic-Republican
AGE AT INAUGURATION - 57
YEARS SERVED - 1801–1809
VICE PRESIDENTS - Aaron Burr, George Clinton
DIED - July 4, 1826, age 83

From 1745 to 1752, Thomas and his family
lived at the Tuckahoe plantation near Richmond, Virginia.

Thomas also attended the Reverend James Maury's **classical school** near Charlottesville, Virginia. He studied long hours and learned to write well. Thomas practiced the violin and learned Greek and Latin.

LAW AND POLITICS

In 1760, Jefferson entered the College of William and Mary in Williamsburg, Virginia. There, he made new friends and read many books. Jefferson was a good student. He often studied up to 15 hours a day! He enjoyed discussing religion, science, and mathematics with his teachers and fellow students.

Jefferson left college after two years. Like most college students of his time, he did not earn a **degree**. For the next five years, he studied law in Williamsburg with Judge George Wythe. Jefferson read law books and observed Wythe in court.

In 1767, Jefferson was admitted to the legal profession. He became a successful lawyer. Two years later, Jefferson was elected to the Virginia legislature. He wrote many laws to help Virginians. Some of these laws were later used in the U.S. **Constitution**. Today, Americans enjoy freedom of religion thanks to Jefferson.

Throughout his life, Jefferson enjoyed learning.

At the College of William and Mary, Jefferson lived in the building that is now called the Sir Christopher Wren Building.

MONTICELLO

In 1768, Jefferson decided to build a house. It would be built on a small hill near Shadwell. Jefferson designed the home himself. He called his estate *Monticello*, which is Italian for "little mountain."

Around this time, Jefferson met Martha Wayles Skelton. Jefferson and Martha loved music. They played songs and sang together. Jefferson and Martha eventually fell in love. They were married on January 1, 1772.

Mr. and Mrs. Jefferson had six children, but only two survived childhood. Martha was born in 1772. Maria was born in 1778.

The Jefferson family lived at Monticello. Both Mr. and Mrs. Jefferson had inherited slaves. Jefferson did not support slavery. But, he depended on slaves to work his farms.

This silhouette is the only known image of Martha Jefferson.

Today, Monticello is a popular tourist attraction for those wishing to learn more about Jefferson.

CONGRESS

Meanwhile, colonists were growing angry with the British government. In 1773, the British placed a tax on tea exports to the colonies. In Boston, Massachusetts, angry colonists protested. They threw 342 chests of British tea into Boston Harbor. This act is called the Boston Tea Party.

The Boston Tea Party helped lead to the American Revolution.

The next year, leaders from the colonies met in Philadelphia, Pennsylvania. They discussed taxes and called for fair treatment from the British government. This meeting is called the First Continental Congress.

Jefferson was ill and did not go to the meeting. But in 1775, he attended the first meeting of the Second Continental Congress. Jefferson firmly believed the colonies should be independent.

The Continental Congress acted as the new government for the colonies. It issued money, set up a postal service, and created a navy. On June 15, Congress chose George Washington to lead the new American army. The **American Revolution** had begun.

Washington served as the army's commander in chief during the American Revolution.

INDEPENDENCE

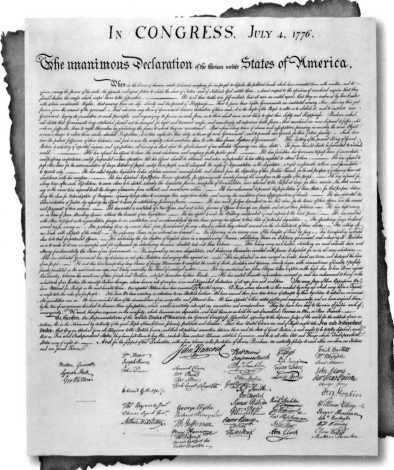

The Declaration of Independence is Jefferson's best-known written work.

In summer 1776, Jefferson was named to an important committee. It was charged with **drafting** a declaration of independence from Great Britain. Jefferson was a talented writer. So, the committee asked him to prepare the document. Jefferson became the chief author of the Declaration of Independence.

The Second Continental Congress met in Independence Hall in Philadelphia. The Declaration of Independence was also signed there.

Congress adopted the Declaration of Independence on July 4. The new document established the United States as an independent nation. And, it declared that the colonies were now independent states. Americans still celebrate the signing of this important document each Fourth of July.

That autumn, Jefferson returned to Virginia. As a Virginia legislator, he worked for better state laws. These laws gave Virginians the right to own land. Virginians also received the right to an education.

Jefferson also worked for religious freedom for all Virginians. In 1777, he wrote the Virginia Statute for Religious Freedom. This act ensured the separation of church and state. It was finally passed in 1786.

In 1779, Jefferson was elected governor of Virginia. He was reelected in 1780. That year,

Jefferson designed the Virginia Capitol in Richmond.

Jefferson moved the state capital from Williamsburg to Richmond. The British army invaded Virginia the next year. Jefferson barely escaped capture. He retired at the end of his term.

On September 6, 1782, Martha Jefferson died. Jefferson was sad and missed his wife. Yet he never remarried.

Hoping to forget his sadness, Jefferson reentered politics. He was elected to serve as a delegate to the Continental Congress. There, he tried to pass laws that would end slavery in new U.S.

territories. Jefferson also proposed to free slaves born in the United States after 1800. But the proposals did not pass.

In 1784, Jefferson went to France as a U.S. diplomat. His daughter Martha went with him. Maria arrived three years later. Jefferson became U.S. minister to France in 1785. He helped spread American business through Europe. He studied European **culture**. And, Jefferson witnessed the start of the **French Revolution**.

The Virginia Capitol was built in 1785, while Jefferson was in France.

TWO NEW PARTIES

While Jefferson was in Paris, France, the U.S. **Constitution** was approved. George Washington became the country's first president. A new U.S. Congress was also elected.

Jefferson returned to America in 1789. President Washington asked Jefferson to join his **cabinet**. Jefferson became the first U.S. **secretary of state**.

Jefferson often argued with Alexander Hamilton, **secretary of the treasury**.

President Washington (far left) *and his cabinet*

20

First page of the U.S. Constitution

Last page of the U.S. Constitution, bearing the signatures of those who approved it

Hamilton was a Federalist. Federalists believed that a strong national government should rule the country.

Jefferson felt that a strong national government was **unconstitutional**. He believed most decisions should be made by states. Jefferson and his supporters opposed the Federalists. So, they formed a new political group called the Democratic-Republican Party.

President Washington sided with Hamilton on many issues. Jefferson grew frustrated. So at the end of 1793, he retired and returned home to Virginia. For the next three years, Jefferson worked at Monticello.

In 1796, it was time to elect a new U.S. president. Jefferson ran as a Democratic-Republican. John Adams ran as a Federalist and won. Jefferson became his vice president.

In 1798, Congress passed the Sedition Act. It became illegal for anyone to criticize the government. Vice President Jefferson called the law unconstitutional. He convinced the Virginia and Kentucky legislatures to vote down

A record of the Electoral College votes from the 1800 election

the law in their states. The Sedition Act **expired** in 1801.

Jefferson again ran for president against Adams in 1800. This time, Jefferson tied fellow Democratic-Republican Aaron Burr. By law, the House of Representatives had to break the tie. The final vote occurred on February 17, 1801. Jefferson was elected the third president of the United States. Burr became his vice president.

Aaron Burr served as vice president from 1801 to 1805. On July 11, 1804, Vice President Burr killed his political rival, Alexander Hamilton, in a duel.

PRESIDENT JEFFERSON

President Jefferson took office on March 4, 1801. He was the first president **inaugurated** at the Capitol in Washington, D.C.

Jefferson worked hard to support the freedoms he believed in. Newspapers printed hateful stories about him. But he did not punish the people who wrote the stories. He thought people should be free to write what they believed. This is called freedom of the press.

President Jefferson helped change laws the Federalists had passed under Adams. He lowered taxes and cut spending for the army and the navy. President Jefferson also removed many Federalists from office.

But there were problems abroad. Pirates often attacked American ships off the North African coast. As commander in chief, Jefferson ordered the U.S. Navy to protect the ships.

President Jefferson's major achievement came in 1803. At that time, France owned

SUPREME COURT APPOINTMENTS

WILLIAM JOHNSON - 1804

HENRY BROCKHOLST LIVINGSTON - 1807

THOMAS TODD - 1807

all the land between the Mississippi River and the Rocky Mountains. This land was called the Louisiana Territory. But France was facing a costly war with Great Britain. France needed to sell the land to make money.

In 1803, the United States extended west to the Mississippi River.

President Jefferson bought the land for the United States. This is called the Louisiana Purchase. The Louisiana Purchase made the United States twice as big.

Jefferson asked Meriwether Lewis and William Clark to explore the new land. The Lewis and Clark Expedition discovered plants and animals never written about before. They made new maps. And, they learned about Native American **cultures**. When they returned, Lewis and Clark told President Jefferson of America's new natural wonders.

The Louisiana Purchase

In 1804, President Jefferson ran for reelection. The Federalist candidate was Charles C. Pinckney. Jefferson easily won reelection. Former governor of New York George Clinton became his vice president.

During his second term, President Jefferson signed the Embargo Act. This act closed all U.S. ports to export shipping. It also stopped imports from Great Britain. As a result of the act, the U.S. **economy** suffered. Jefferson also stopped a **conspiracy** by former vice president Burr. Burr had attempted to create a new nation in the western territories.

In 1808, the Democratic-Republicans wanted President Jefferson to run for a third term. He refused. Jefferson felt being president should not be a lifelong job. Instead, he helped James Madison win the election. When Madison took office in 1809, Jefferson retired to Monticello.

PRESIDENT JEFFERSON'S CABINET

FIRST TERM
MARCH 4, 1801–
MARCH 4, 1805

- **STATE –** James Madison
- **TREASURY –** Samuel Dexter
   Albert Gallatin (from May 14, 1801)
- **WAR –** Henry Dearborn
- **NAVY –** Benjamin Stoddert
   Robert Smith (from July 27, 1801)
- **ATTORNEY GENERAL –** Levi Lincoln

SECOND TERM
MARCH 4, 1805–
MARCH 4, 1809

- **STATE –** James Madison
- **TREASURY –** Albert Gallatin
- **WAR –** Henry Dearborn
- **NAVY –** Robert Smith
- **ATTORNEY GENERAL –** John Breckinridge
   Caesar A. Rodney
   (from January 20, 1807)

IN RETIREMENT

At Monticello, Jefferson kept busy. He spent time with friends and family. He drew up more plans for the house and the gardens. Jefferson also wrote letters, read books, and did science projects.

During the **War of 1812**, British soldiers burned the Library of Congress. So in 1815, Jefferson sold Congress his personal library. Then, he started collecting more books.

In 1819, Jefferson started the University of Virginia. He designed the buildings, hired the staff, and chose the textbooks. The school opened in March 1825 with 40 students.

On July 4, 1826, Thomas Jefferson died. He was 83. Former president John Adams died the same day. It was exactly 50 years after the adoption of the Declaration of Independence. Jefferson is buried at Monticello.

Jefferson wrote the inscription for his gravestone. It reads, "Here was buried Thomas Jefferson, Author of the Declaration of American Independence, of the Statute of Virginia for Religious Freedom, and Father of the University of Virginia."

Jefferson led America through a period of growth and prosperity. He is remembered for his many contributions to U.S. history. His most well-known accomplishment is authoring the Declaration of Independence.

In 1943, the Jefferson Memorial in Washington, D.C., was completed. Jefferson's likeness is also carved into Mount Rushmore in South Dakota. Thomas Jefferson is remembered as one of America's most accomplished founders.

Jefferson Memorial in Washington, D.C.

OFFICE OF THE PRESIDENT

BRANCHES OF GOVERNMENT

The U.S. government is divided into three branches. They are the executive, legislative, and judicial branches. This division is called a separation of powers. Each branch has some power over the others. This is called a system of checks and balances.

EXECUTIVE BRANCH

The executive branch enforces laws. It is made up of the president, the vice president, and the president's cabinet. The president represents the United States around the world. He or she oversees relations with other countries and signs treaties. The president signs bills into law and appoints officials and federal judges. He or she also leads the military and manages government workers.

LEGISLATIVE BRANCH

The legislative branch makes laws, maintains the military, and regulates trade. It also has the power to declare war. This branch consists of the Senate and the House of Representatives. Together, these two houses make up Congress. Each state has two senators. A state's population determines the number of representatives it has.

JUDICIAL BRANCH

The judicial branch interprets laws. It consists of district courts, courts of appeals, and the Supreme Court. District courts try cases. If a person disagrees with a trial's outcome, he or she may appeal. If the courts of appeals support the ruling, a person may appeal to the Supreme Court. The Supreme Court also makes sure that laws follow the U.S. Constitution.

QUALIFICATIONS FOR OFFICE

To be president, a person must meet three requirements. A candidate must be at least 35 years old and a natural-born U.S. citizen. He or she must also have lived in the United States for at least 14 years.

ELECTORAL COLLEGE

The U.S. presidential election is an indirect election. Voters from each state choose electors to represent them in the Electoral College. The number of electors from each state is based on population. Each elector has one electoral vote. Electors are pledged to cast their vote for the candidate who receives the highest number of popular votes in their state. A candidate must receive the majority of Electoral College votes to win.

TERM OF OFFICE

Each president may be elected to two four-year terms. Sometimes, a president may only be elected once. This happens if he or she served more than two years of the previous president's term.

The presidential election is held on the Tuesday after the first Monday in November. The president is sworn in on January 20 of the following year. At that time, he or she takes the oath of office:

I do solemnly swear (or affirm) that I will faithfully execute the office of President of the United States, and will to the best of my ability, preserve, protect and defend the Constitution of the United States.

LINE OF SUCCESSION

The Presidential Succession Act of 1947 defines who becomes president if the president cannot serve. The vice president is first in the line of succession. Next are the Speaker of the House and the President Pro Tempore of the Senate. If none of these individuals is able to serve, the office falls to the president's cabinet members. They would take office in the order in which each department was created:

Secretary of State

Secretary of the Treasury

Secretary of Defense

Attorney General

Secretary of the Interior

Secretary of Agriculture

Secretary of Commerce

Secretary of Labor

Secretary of Health and Human Services

Secretary of Housing and Urban Development

Secretary of Transportation

Secretary of Energy

Secretary of Education

Secretary of Veterans Affairs

Secretary of Homeland Security

BENEFITS

- While in office, the president receives a salary of $400,000 each year. He or she lives in the White House and has 24-hour Secret Service protection.

- The president may travel on a Boeing 747 jet called Air Force One. The airplane can accommodate 70 passengers. It has kitchens, a dining room, sleeping areas, and a conference room. It also has fully equipped offices with the latest communications systems. Air Force One can fly halfway around the world before needing to refuel. It can even refuel in flight!

- If the president wishes to travel by car, he or she uses Cadillac One. Cadillac One is a Cadillac Deville. It has been modified with heavy armor and communications systems. The president takes Cadillac One along when visiting other countries if secure transportation will be needed.

- The president also travels on a helicopter called Marine One. Like the presidential car, Marine One accompanies the president when traveling abroad if necessary.

- Sometimes, the president needs to get away and relax with family and friends. Camp David is the official presidential retreat. It is located in the cool, wooded mountains in Maryland. The U.S. Navy maintains the retreat, and the U.S. Marine Corps keeps it secure. The camp offers swimming, tennis, golf, and hiking.

- When the president leaves office, he or she receives Secret Service protection for ten more years. He or she also receives a yearly pension of $191,300 and funding for office space, supplies, and staff.

PRESIDENTS AND THEIR TERMS

PRESIDENT	PARTY	TOOK OFFICE	LEFT OFFICE	TERMS SERVED	VICE PRESIDENT
George Washington	None	April 30, 1789	March 4, 1797	Two	John Adams
John Adams	Federalist	March 4, 1797	March 4, 1801	One	Thomas Jefferson
Thomas Jefferson	Democratic-Republican	March 4, 1801	March 4, 1809	Two	Aaron Burr, George Clinton
James Madison	Democratic-Republican	March 4, 1809	March 4, 1817	Two	George Clinton, Elbridge Gerry
James Monroe	Democratic-Republican	March 4, 1817	March 4, 1825	Two	Daniel D. Tompkins
John Quincy Adams	Democratic-Republican	March 4, 1825	March 4, 1829	One	John C. Calhoun
Andrew Jackson	Democrat	March 4, 1829	March 4, 1837	Two	John C. Calhoun, Martin Van Buren
Martin Van Buren	Democrat	March 4, 1837	March 4, 1841	One	Richard M. Johnson
William H. Harrison	Whig	March 4, 1841	April 4, 1841	Died During First Term	John Tyler
John Tyler	Whig	April 6, 1841	March 4, 1845	Completed Harrison's Term	Office Vacant
James K. Polk	Democrat	March 4, 1845	March 4, 1849	One	George M. Dallas
Zachary Taylor	Whig	March 5, 1849	July 9, 1850	Died During First Term	Millard Fillmore

PRESIDENT	PARTY	TOOK OFFICE	LEFT OFFICE	TERMS SERVED	VICE PRESIDENT
Millard Fillmore	Whig	July 10, 1850	March 4, 1853	Completed Taylor's Term	Office Vacant
Franklin Pierce	Democrat	March 4, 1853	March 4, 1857	One	William R.D. King
James Buchanan	Democrat	March 4, 1857	March 4, 1861	One	John C. Breckinridge
Abraham Lincoln	Republican	March 4, 1861	April 15, 1865	Served One Term, Died During Second Term	Hannibal Hamlin, Andrew Johnson
Andrew Johnson	Democrat	April 15, 1865	March 4, 1869	Completed Lincoln's Second Term	Office Vacant
Ulysses S. Grant	Republican	March 4, 1869	March 4, 1877	Two	Schuyler Colfax, Henry Wilson
Rutherford B. Hayes	Republican	March 3, 1877	March 4, 1881	One	William A. Wheeler
James A. Garfield	Republican	March 4, 1881	September 19, 1881	Died During First Term	Chester Arthur
Chester Arthur	Republican	September 20, 1881	March 4, 1885	Completed Garfield's Term	Office Vacant
Grover Cleveland	Democrat	March 4, 1885	March 4, 1889	One	Thomas A. Hendricks
Benjamin Harrison	Republican	March 4, 1889	March 4, 1893	One	Levi P. Morton
Grover Cleveland	Democrat	March 4, 1893	March 4, 1897	One	Adlai E. Stevenson
William McKinley	Republican	March 4, 1897	September 14, 1901	Served One Term, Died During Second Term	Garret A. Hobart, Theodore Roosevelt

PRESIDENTS 13–25, 1850–1901

PRESIDENT	PARTY	TOOK OFFICE	LEFT OFFICE	TERMS SERVED	VICE PRESIDENT
Theodore Roosevelt	Republican	September 14, 1901	March 4, 1909	Completed McKinley's Second Term, Served One Term	Office Vacant, Charles Fairbanks
William Taft	Republican	March 4, 1909	March 4, 1913	One	James S. Sherman
Woodrow Wilson	Democrat	March 4, 1913	March 4, 1921	Two	Thomas R. Marshall
Warren G. Harding	Republican	March 4, 1921	August 2, 1923	Died During First Term	Calvin Coolidge
Calvin Coolidge	Republican	August 3, 1923	March 4, 1929	Completed Harding's Term, Served One Term	Office Vacant, Charles Dawes
Herbert Hoover	Republican	March 4, 1929	March 4, 1933	One	Charles Curtis
Franklin D. Roosevelt	Democrat	March 4, 1933	April 12, 1945	Served Three Terms, Died During Fourth Term	John Nance Garner, Henry A. Wallace, Harry S. Truman
Harry S. Truman	Democrat	April 12, 1945	January 20, 1953	Completed Roosevelt's Fourth Term, Served One Term	Office Vacant, Alben Barkley
Dwight D. Eisenhower	Republican	January 20, 1953	January 20, 1961	Two	Richard Nixon
John F. Kennedy	Democrat	January 20, 1961	November 22, 1963	Died During First Term	Lyndon B. Johnson
Lyndon B. Johnson	Democrat	November 22, 1963	January 20, 1969	Completed Kennedy's Term, Served One Term	Office Vacant, Hubert H. Humphrey
Richard Nixon	Republican	January 20, 1969	August 9, 1974	Completed First Term, Resigned During Second Term	Spiro T. Agnew, Gerald Ford

PRESIDENTS 26–37, 1901–1974

PRESIDENT	PARTY	TOOK OFFICE	LEFT OFFICE	TERMS SERVED	VICE PRESIDENT
Gerald Ford	Republican	August 9, 1974	January 20, 1977	Completed Nixon's Second Term	Nelson A. Rockefeller
Jimmy Carter	Democrat	January 20, 1977	January 20, 1981	One	Walter Mondale
Ronald Reagan	Republican	January 20, 1981	January 20, 1989	Two	George H.W. Bush
George H.W. Bush	Republican	January 20, 1989	January 20, 1993	One	Dan Quayle
Bill Clinton	Democrat	January 20, 1993	January 20, 2001	Two	Al Gore
George W. Bush	Republican	January 20, 2001	January 20, 2009	Two	Dick Cheney
Barack Obama	Democrat	January 20, 2009			Joe Biden

"I cannot live without books." Thomas Jefferson

WRITE TO THE PRESIDENT

You may write to the president at:

**The White House
1600 Pennsylvania Avenue NW
Washington, DC 20500**

You may e-mail the president at:
comments@whitehouse.gov

PRESIDENTS 38–44, 1974–

GLOSSARY

American Revolution - from 1775 to 1783. A war for independence between Great Britain and its North American colonies. The colonists won and created the United States of America.

cabinet - a group of advisers chosen by the president to lead government departments.

classical school - a school that provided instruction in literature, art, and life of ancient Greece and Rome.

conspiracy - a secret agreement to do an unlawful or wrongful act.

Constitution - the laws that govern the United States.

culture - the customs, arts, and tools of a nation or people at a certain time.

degree - a title given by a college to its graduates after they have completed their studies.

draft - to compose or prepare.

economy - the way a nation uses its money, goods, and natural resources.

expire - to come to an end.

French Revolution - revolutionary movement in France between 1787 and 1799.

inaugurate (ih-NAW-gyuh-rayt) - to swear into a political office.

secretary of state - a member of the president's cabinet who handles relations with other countries.

secretary of the treasury - a member of the president's cabinet that heads the U.S. Department of the Treasury. The secretary advises the president on financial policies and reports to Congress on the nation's finances. The secretary of the treasury is the U.S. government's chief financial officer.

tutor - to teach a student privately. The teacher is also called a tutor.

unconstitutional - something that goes against the laws of a constitution.

War of 1812 - from 1812 to 1814. A war fought between the United States and Great Britain over shipping rights and the capture of U.S. soldiers.

WEB SITES

To learn more about Thomas Jefferson, visit ABDO Publishing Company on the World Wide Web at **www.abdopublishing.com.** Web sites about Thomas Jefferson are featured on our Book Links page. These links are routinely monitored and updated to provide the most current information available.

INDEX